Poetic Blazons
From Africa

Misheck P. Chingozha

Langaa Research & Publishing CIG
Mankon, Bamenda

Publisher
Langaa RPCIG
Langaa Research & Publishing Common Initiative Group
P.O. Box 902 Mankon
Bamenda
North West Region
Cameroon
Langaagrp@gmail.com
www.langaa-rpcig.net

Distributed in and outside N. America by African Books Collective
orders@africanbookscollective.com
www.africanbookscollective.com

ISBN-10: 9956-764-71-X

ISBN-13: 978-9956-764-71-6

Table of Contents

Preface

How I loathed poetry at school, all to go and write poetic rhymes to my young lovers past high school days! How am overjoyed to foreword this poetic anthology that describes a time in the life of a son of the soil – an African child, past and present. This piece of literature in your hands tells of a great poetic work – a story that transverse languages, ethnic boundaries, cultures and continents. Written in a simplistic, albeit deep language, the layout speaks of an author who is in touch with nature. His use of a simple but poetic language is even more intriguing as it often calls for his artistic creative metaphors of his own genius. Who said the Queen's language was not dynamic?

This anthology, a compilation that dates back to the early 1990s (an era well-known for the notorious ESAP!), relevantly grapples with contemporary issues, seen not by an ordinary eye, but one with an in-depth epistemic metaphysical analysis of past and present. Raised by a single mother, Chingozha, in his own words here stands to attest the plight of a child strolling the savanna woodlands of rural Africa and a child lying on the dusty streets of urban Africa. His primary school experiences in three provinces of Zimbabwe as a result of a broken family spoken in the poetic language, narrates a common story by one of those who have stood to defy the odds all thanks to a strong mother, who, albeit passed on without seeing this project coming into fruition, inspired the pencilling of this work.

Skilfully scripted, this beautiful work takes you through a universal language, the language of nature that touches on plains, vleis, the savanna woodlands, the mountains, the hills, oceans and beaches paradoxically by one who has spent most of his days in a landlocked Zimbabwe! His love for the birds' species come natural, summarily with themes of love, subtle politics, death, life struggles, heroism and hope.. Deeply moved by his experiences, the author tailors words of virtue, encouragement, honesty, trust, responsibility, values, manners and courage juxtaposed against greed, hypocrisy, deceit, unfaithfulness, and laziness all in a language that crosses natural and social sciences.

A poetic piece that sinks deep into the chasm of Africa's cosmogony is conveniently introduced by one piece that preaches hope. In the introductory work "Once beaten" one cannot help but notice the message of hope addressing a people and continent that has been ravaged all by natural and anthropogenic disasters. This theme resonates well with what the author goes on to share, on a personal, intra-personal and inter-personal experiences at both local and global levels. This anthology is holistic. It speaks to you all: a scorned lover, a lover, an African orphan, an HIV and AIDS victim, persons living with disabilities, a losing political candidate, and a victim of any form of abuse, the seemingly less recognised professional, a regretting teenager and indeed the policy maker and bureaucrat in the corridors of power.

The terrestrial approach in the "Flying sparrows" gives a gloomy picture of the world as we know it, the only hope awakened by the great piece that preaches the "despair not" message, a message of determination, a message of hope, a messages that plants firmness to all and sundry amidst all the chaos, humanly and divinely. I could not stand but be imbued in the patriotic feelings and continental morale overwhelmingly oozing out through "Africa Our

Motherland" with the background of UB40's "Sing our own Song" playing in the background. Cutting themes of Ubuntu, overtones of religion, and undertones of patriarchy loom large is this piece.

Tasked to foreword this work, I was quick to accept, having not done so for a poetic assortment. Thanks to Dr. Phil's encouragement that "The moment that opportunity knocks is not the time to be overcome with humility, self-effacement, and self-doubt." I had to "take it, to make it" and it worked out well for me. Indulge in this poetic collection as a rookie and you will emerge, having gone through the depth of a far distant glimmer of hope, a re-energised and re-invented individual with the zeal and zest to fly high in spite of your past and present circumstances.

Jobert Ngwenya
Founding Director:
Jobert Ngwenya Opportunities Foundation
Speaker, Youth Coach, Writer, Researcher, Educator

Once Beaten...

When you recover from blows of yesterday
Rise to up the mountain top
From such height conceive new strategies
Enduring strategies
Descend forth and keep pace with the rest
But cautious and vigilant
For monsters prey on hearts
Hearts that would cultivate life
And hold it till breaking point

When your emotions are really exasperated
Do not explode untimely
Be calculative
Lower your head below the tide
And swim to the island
From there establish a fort
And recruit a defence regiment
Keep guard and alert

When sea blindness impair your vision
Like tortoise withdraw to your shell
Leave them trample on you
Endure and let them feel you are a rock
When all appears clear and warm
Shoot from your shell with a start
At double tortoise speed
Remain conscious of what surrounds you

Remain on guard all seasons
And ascertain on their return they meet a fortress

If you allowed them to hit again
That would be disheartening
Evade second blows
Be beaten once and never again
Once beaten, twice shy.

Roses Are Flowers

Breathlessly at noon I squat
With deep memories heightened
I critically take a view amid mist
But abreast the wild and weird clings

I gather energies and strength
And jump across fences and rivers
Numbness cripples and drowns
All my dreams, hopes and aspirations

With the head above the waters
The dolphin communicates in a distance
I promise not to get wet
And swim to the sea shore
To see the show on the beach
And deal with all challenges thrust
With the trust to keep my journey north
Noting I still have a cause to exonerate

When the troding knight notices
With a merciful heart I get a ride
Across Knights-bridge into a better world
A world with vast stretches of grasslands
Such grass that unveil a sight inviting
A sight that encourages and upholds life
Such a wish from childhood
When I could see bees fly
When I could see bees search for nectar
When I could see bees in swarms

As they flew past our dagga hut
With brief spells of rest on our roof
I would be scared to death
And sweat till soaked like damped in the Mississipi waters

Across knights bridge I sit
Head between knees
Tears roll down and soften the tormented heart
Perturbed with the echoes in the east
I rise with a start
I amble towards Mount Hampden
To seek some comfort and rest

But Hope

On the way the weird trail
The worst assail even the mute and numb
But hope if maintained, will the goal be attained
All but determination in this harshy and cruel world pays
Fall today, drown today, limp today
Eat not your heart up, despair not
Rise looking ahead and fortify your mansion
Watch the world around as it rotates
Firm your stance with the sword shining
And walk ahead determined and hopeful

Tormented Soul

Reproachfully I amble back
But in vain try to understand
I tighten my already tight grip
But no echoes wail

With some little comfort descending
I thrive multtimes over
Still left, right and centre
Missiles impactfully hit
But on regaining consciousness
I double the pace in anticipation of lighter sorrows
With the heart in tatters and exhausted
Tears downpour like torrentials
And wounds of blame ache bitterly

As the faints of hope flash
I collect my crumbled structure
But no energy prompts movement
Thus the heart bleeds even more

Soul Robbery

With deep sorrow and astonishment
We learnt of the robbery
When such a blow we least anticipated
Right to narrow the pain cut
To beneath the sea bed the hearts sunk
And tears painfully rolled down
Realising the obvious gap
The gap that will perpetuate

With untold pain of loss
All converged in pain and sympathy
To pay their last respects to the man
Our benefactor and force to reckon
A man who had love and cause
And fought tirelessly with all zeal and zest
To see our being flourish and prosper
A man of integrity and purpose
A man of prowess and diligence
A man whose works we will remember
But today peacefully at rest

He was strongly willed a man
A man with principles
A man with the credentials and power
But today in pain of loss
We glare up and down
For an answer never to come
For earth cruelly engulfed
All his wits and mettle

Your voice will echo always
Sending stimuli to review your works
Your name will vividly stay
And forever live in the hearts of many
Your work will forever shine Guy
Your unique ways will forever be appreciated
Though earth cruelly engulfed you

In you was a leader
A teacher with love for the people
Who fought with all zest?
Determined for the single minded goal
To see us grow and prosper
Rest in peace

The Will To Love

If the power to command, I had
If the power over the life I have, I had
Birds I would command to sing my songs to you
The songs pronounced not
But deep down
The songs that tell my story
The story making my life today
The life that is making meaning I credit
The credit that makes me feel the change
Such a change great and incredible
Praying the shadow of night
Will not have voices
The voices of rage and jealous that see no good
And thwart even the blooming rose

The Real Me

Unmoved and unshaken
I will remain firm and strong
Upholding my cause and principles
Without hesitance I'll lead ahead
Up in arms with ill influences
Thus remain the real me

With the last inch of my sword
I'll fight, fight alone
To remain me
And the real person in me
A battle it may be
For the hurricane, winds are strong
But all alone, as a man
Boast less but principled
I'll stand the colossial forces
As a man with cause and purpose
Alertness of who serpents are
Dominate the front
Thus I'll live
The real person in me

Sparrows Sing

Have you ever drowned in an nth deep pool
And no hand was stretched to save you?
Have you ever been bewildered and tormented
And you had none to turn to?
Have you ever had some beautiful joy and lovely whisper
But you had none to share it with?
Have you ever been in a precarious position and trapped
And you still had to recover and keep agoing on your own
Have you ever wanted to talk
But there was none to listen?
Have you ever wanted to share some experience and
memoirs
But on turning you realise you are the sole figure?
Have you ever cherished to hear some voice
But no assurance and comfort descended?
Have you ever felt dejected and cursed
And like water tears streamed down?
Have you ever felt unwanted and unfortunate
And you searched for comfort in the middle of the night?
Have you ever had tears corroding your cheeks
When you had been a victim of circumstances?
Have you ever been torn apart,
And there was no reassurance and resurrection of the
dampen spirit?
Have you ever wanted to cry
But for some reason immediately stopped?
Have you ever wanted to give up
But kept going because no one would damn care?

Yes sparrows sing in my garden
Beautiful songs in summer
But winter sends them across seas and oceans
When I would wish the songs persist
Sparrows inspire and give hope
Days come and go
But the songs echo at all times

As I stroll in my garden at dawn
I remain captivated to the melodies
Melodies that send a stimuli, meaning and comfort
But sparrows leave for the east

When I gaze in the north
The flock bow in respect at a distance
And tunes sweetly stretch across the land
When I amble back in pain
The echo tickles my heart
I return to the garden with hope
But the remaining flock fly to the west
I wait for their return at dusk
When their return will bring comfort

Children Of God

Children of God we are
Boys, girls and all
Children of God we are
Young, old and unborn
Children of God we are
Abled, disabled and all
Children of God we are
 And forever we shall

On My Last Lap

From far and wide
All I associated with converge
With untold pain of loss
They relate our beautiful past
But there I remain silent
As though I'll not appreciate
They grieve and talk good
May be, mere praises
But I'll not murmur a word
On my last lap I'll be peaceful
Reviewing my works
A gap unveils
But not even a multitude wishes
Will give back the life
I'll perpetually miss
Condolences will pour
But my circle will be complete
On my last lap
Their hearts will sink
A tense atmosphere will prevail
The grievous faces will look up and down
As though in prayer for my second coming
But poor friends- I'm not another Jesus
The smiles shared yesterday
Will be no more
As they pay their last respects
On my last lap

Flying Sparrows

When I'm above hills and mountains
With my eyes alert and open fully
I see clearly all that would be concealed
I hear all whispers, talks and cries

When I fly above hills and mountains
My sympathy is provoked
When I see wilting leaves fall
And starving children die

When I'm flying with my colours bright
I wish I could take all life with me
As I see innocent life sweating, crying and starving
While no remedy in sight and unveiling

When I'm above hills and mountains
With my tormented heart pounding and breaking
I see the foul play, pretence and cheating among men,
And wish I could come down to put a stop to it

At height I sing and praise loudly,
I pray that mercy descend on earth,
I see all evils that man cannot conceal
The real evils of mankind

When I'm above hills and mountains
I see the damage from falling rocks
I hear the cracking sound of the life falling apart
And wish I could come down to put a stop to it

Wishing I could help
 But sadly I cannot.

Tough Tale

As the cyclone ravage the serenity of the night
Willy nilly tears of pain roll down
When breaking branches fall
And dove eggs break
With screams and pain a fort is built
To conquer all odds
To suppress adding ills unveiling
Revealing disaster and sorrow
But with dust and down pours
Eyes are blinded and vision impaired
Thus the worst assails

With crowing, hooting and swaying
The heart softens
And from hide I come
Singing the evils of the cyclone
Sparrows congregate in the baobab
Hawks rally and tears fall,
Tears of pain-reveal pain
Such pain to marrow
But tomorrow answers not
As the plea hits skies
And the plight echo audibly

Rolling Stone

Like a rolling stone
Dusk came with meagre harvest
Cries echoed across skies
And all life wilted and bowed
Not in respect but mourning

Time went by
With no cause realised
Now the mind drowns in hustles
While the hippocampus will hardly work out why,
But a rolling stone gathers no moss

At dawn ego shined
Pride sprouted noticeably
And astray a journey made
Such a journey not applauded
But the thalamus will not recall why all starve
At crucial a time
When life would have been sweet
All fingers pointed yesterday
Caused no remorse

Only but today when all underneath criy
But crucification repudiated
While prayers for pardon and guidance are pronounced
Will some change be evident
But time waits not for any
A minute lost never will be regained
A rolling stone also wishes
Had I stopped in my teens

Life would have been different

Derailed Virtue

Even in the merciless sun
Little unveiled meaning
And I still enjoyed my swim

In the east at night
Came a trodding knight
Shining and preaching
Such teachings disguised

Behind the baobab
Came songs and whispers
Whispers warning and comforting
But the message went past

From behind the hill
Cries wailed through skies
And like fragments piercing
The truth went past

Convinced and determined negatively
I made an oath
And astray headed not looking back

A new creation I was
With old self discarded
And new resolutions set
But derailing the credit worth known past

The Heart In Tatters

When the heart is in tatters
And psychological stress is heightened
Unveil from your shell

When the heart is depressed and agonised
Be bold and fight uncompromisingly
Lead ahead with no turn backs

When your happiness they rob
And your pride they destroy
Turn around and keep distant

When your chances they cruelly barricade
Leave no stone unturned
Fight to repossess yours rightfully

When at night the knight assails
Be wary and stand firm
Fight with all your energy

When you speak but remain unheard
Do not break and get discouraged
Keep your head above the tide and swim

When the dolphin summons
Swim to the deeper waters
Listen, adopt and implement ideas received

When the world seems to jeer
Remain yourself and hopeful

Remembering slumps come and go

Be a man, bold and conscious
In summer, autumn, winter and spring
And at all times on earth

Changing Times

When the wind blows
All trees respectfully sway
When the sun comes
All live growing leaves dry up

When summer comes
All trees shine beautifully
But when winter follows
All life and glamour disappears yet again,

When summer returns again
New leaves shine and flowers bloom
But winter again
Jealously bring them down

When summer comes
Rains fall again crops grow, flowers blossom
But winter dries all land and chicks hurdle for warmth
As times continue to change

Tormented Heart

As I contemplated under the acacia shade
Thoughts of yesterday vividly unveiled
Impairing any beaming chances for glory
For the inherent fear in hibernation

Sweat oozed and streamed
Soaking wholly my tattered clothes
As no comfort descended
I would leave it to time

My poor heart bled
Subsequently causing cardiac arrest
But no team would rescue
Only time would entangle the knot

Sounds in the East stole
Momentarily my meditation
I sighed with relief
But short lived it was with no new chapters unveiling.

With the thorny pain growing
I rose with a start
Glared in the North
But it was not time yet

The time was distant
Though I wished time soon
Time had the answer
And I had to leave it to time
And today await the time

Bleeding Heart

Like a hot sharp rod reality pierced through
The heart bled and crumbled
And life never would be the same

Least when anticipated the blow struck
Breaking the jaws and maiming
But not even tears would forge change

Amazing how prolonged and short night can become
When in a vacuum one glares and gazes
But fold and wait for an answer never to come

In the shadows of night in pain
Echoes wail and disturb the serenity
But that damage gravely rooted

As night disappears and dawn approaches
I remain mute and shivering
For fear of starting all over again

Tormenting to see the fall it was
But side stepped in grave pain
For no evasion and reversion unveiled

The pain and damage would live
The heart would always reproach
But no change would surface

It pains and itches the brain
It damages and detriments the brain

But even the worst can be welcome

Bona fide chapters had unclasped
Chapters portraying tomorrow and yesterday
But today no yield, but a harvest of thorns

Blooming Rose

Like a bee in nectary search
My heart wandered across plains and vleis
But no rest came

Patience and perseverance paid
When the pace I doubled
And the effort I trebled
At down the blooming rose unveiled

The heart would now rest
The answer to life had manifested
Exhibiting changes of that new era
The era that had total transformation

Looking at the blooming rose
I had no doubt even at night
What I saw in the blooming rose
The heart was content and would hold

I would enhance all hope now
I would invest all dreams now
I would do everything for it now
Till time lapsed

The blooming rose wholly stole my heart
And concealed it in the ovary
Like the ovules developing into seed
The relationship will grow by day

The blooming rose shall reign
The blooming rose shall shine
The blooming rose shall be watered
The blooming rose shall be managed
Thus retain the sweetness and unique tenderness

Snake In The Grass

Sweetly whispers as a friend would
Embraces warmly like a mother would
While his score burning
And will echo as a thundery blow

Like chicks hurdle when winter comes
You may when the worst assails
With a free mind and think you are friends
Yes, you may be-but what kind of friends?

Time may swiftly roll by
While you brisk hand in hand
All as lure, sadly
And time finds you trapped
Enclosed in an iron net
A net harsh and suffocating
Pinning you once and for all
Be wary of the snake in the grass

Still Human

If I were a weaver bird
I would fly without perching
If but persuaded by a female
Only would I build a home
If home not approved
That would spell my fate
I would fly above again
With no come backs
With no worries
Except for my caring neighbour
I would sing my love songs
Though my heart will not accept a female
Once broken a heart mends not
So is mine
Broken it is, and I'll stay
Some will love
But I'll not melt and embrace
Some will embrace and entice
But I would rather sing
Such songs telling my history
"I wanted a female…
I wanted offsprings of my own…
But my nest was not approved"
To heights I will fly
As long I'm still me
But hate myself if woed again
For once if beaten
Twice shy

Seasons

As the seasons change
My mind follows steadily
And never cease to hope
For it is in hope fruits bear

As the new season unfold
I fold my arms and bow
Patiently I wait, hopefully
I hear the course and way forward

As another season comes
With all my heart I welcome.
And soon come to understand what it brings
For seasons come and go

Seasons unveil different courses
Thus we have hotness, coldness, dampness
All coming in a row
And memories drastically change

Seasons bring joy and cries,
They bring beauty and crashes
Chilling and hurdling also come with seasons
As rattling, sweating and down pours

Season should be taken as they come
Adapt to the sudden changes, be bold and stead fast
Where harshness heightens firm the grip
And where warmness manifests embrace warmly
Realising seasons descend with a myriad of variations

Examination Time

The best time to tell it all
The time that decides and confirms
The moment that demarcates and separates
The time that pronounces failure and crowns greatness
And the time that pains or soothes

Brains gather during this time
To breaking point stretch
To the last particle function
All but to attain the best

The time tickles fast as though but to salute my downfall
With 30 minutes left I perspire
With 15 minutes I panick
With 10 minutes I gather courage to accept defeat
With 5 minutes turmoil strikes
At zero time I mourn bitterly
And stop to say
Oh! I have to start all over again…!!

Stand Firm

When a dark cloud descends
And the serenity is ravaged
Squat and contemplate
For resolutions rekindle the heart

When the bleeding heart weighs
Evasion of the black past becomes imminent
But the past evil rise to even greater heights
Yet the mansion has to be fortified

At sunrise, prune and bury
Make strides in the North
Retain hope and resuscitate
All avenues and revamp

When the hibiscus are blooming
And the hills remain still keep ears to the ground
As the fall army worm invades
All fields and destroy life, retain hope

When in day light cocaine they trade
And bribes herald and telecast
Swim under water
But do not get wet

When the sharks befriend
Consult the dolphin
Look to the East
And scout for climbers

Poor Duck

Like a busy bee
In nectary search
I explored all avenues
Went down valleys
And up in mountains
With the grass green
And flowers blooming
My face beamed

Upon the born-hardt
Lay an answer
Thicketed the path was
Into my flesh thorns pricked
But I would reach
With zest and comfort
Determined for the single minded goal
I walked ahead
In the world far, laughter echoed
And optimism firmed root

I persisted with pain
The fruit I cherished
But trodding the path painful
Harder I tried
But till today
I stand awaiting the unknown

Africa Our Motherland

Africa, our motherland, Africa
You have no cause for remorse
But a continent to regain
Thus firmly stand and fight
To emancipate yourself
From the bondage,
Enslaving you night and day

Across the land the cries echo
From your children dying
Children denied of their Godly right to be free
By no natural power but fellow men
Men like you and me
Men born of a woman
But for material gains and superiority
Let blood shed herald and telecast

Stand firm Africa
Ahead of you lies a task
Thus shelve your mercy and realise your cause
Break the meaningless and unreasonable bounds Africa
Fight to the best of your ability
To entangle the vicious knot
Implanted by killers, bloody seekers
Non progressiveness and surrogate forces
To destabilise your serenity and sweetness
Fight on Africa, fight on

Call for total commitment Africa
Have your sons and daughters involved

Yes from Cape town to Cairo
Resurrect the almost dampen spirits
Ascertain a day awaits
But for now patience, courage and sacrifice
For now resolve, resilience and persistence

It pains and itches
It disturbs and worries
But for how long?
For how long shall we cry brothers
For how long shall tears corrode our cheeks?
For how long shall our faces wear and tear
In mourning the evils we face
For how long shall violence make headlines?
For how long shall we die in numbers?
Bruished, pushed and die in innocence
For no justification under the sun
For how long shall we let go
Without the scantiest challenge thrust
Africa! You have men and women
Real Powerful and intelligent men and witful women
Man like I am, woman like she is
Unite and fight on

For how long shall the significance of skin, religion and
status prevail?
Thwarting our chances for glory as a family
Brothers, courage and sacrifice
Courage and sacrifice alone
Banners should fly sky high
Courage and sacrifice

For how long shall manslaughter
Dominate our papers and transistors
For how long shall blacks,
All blacks be 'black' charcoal black
And down trodden
For how long?
For how long brothers?

Africa unite
Let all your children come under the brotherhood umbrella
And let peace descend in Africa
Africa, our motherland
We're are all your children
White, black, coloured and whoever
We are all children of God
We are your children
We are descendants of Abraham
Thus no man is more equal than the other
No man has the right to murder
No man has the right to slave
No man has the right to physically abuse
Mentally torture and sexually harass
No man has the right to
Plunder resources

Africa unite for no man has the right to loot
Africa live
Africa our motherland Africa

Real Love

As night falls
I gaze up in the sky
To see shining stars
And see the comfort to lead ahead
But the poor heart takes it not
With the serenity of night creeping
The pain pierces through my nerves
Realising I miss her

Glaring in the north
I see the shadows of night
And wish one could bring her
To ease the pain in me
But all night I grieve
Realising love is painful

As morning approaches
I notice light engulf the darkness
And think she'll appear to comfort
But the distance allows not
Looking at the rising sun
I feel it will bring her from the East but throughout day
I miss her

As I take a walk
Around the fields in green
I think of how important it is
To find the company entertaining
To find the relationship passionate
To find the time together splendid

And realising the hearts
Are growing in love
As the noon rays hit the landscape
Sweat oozes
As though to cool my burning heart
Lamenting, I close my eyes
But no comfort unveils

In my heart I read chapters
True chapters telling my feelings
Such chapters to say:-
I love honestly and genuinely
I have real passionate love
I do wholly
In a manner never before
I accept totally

Moment Of Truth

With no friends abreast
I collected the remains of my body
I revisited the path of my life
And dull events unfolded
I looked down in regret
Tears rolling down
As I came to terms with reality
My last day had come

Boomerang

Slowly I weather and tear
The bugs bore and suck night and day
As I see night disappearing
And day light creeping in,
My days roll by painfully

Boastful and strongly willed
I was, not long
Today, tears corrode my cheeks
Perspiration soak my pants,
I will not last

Jovial and myopic I was,
Not long it was
But today I mourn
Though with myself to wholly reproach

In untold pain
All my evil boomerang
Watchful I see it gallop
But numbness entangles tightly
And with the head down
I fall and let none sympathise

I'll not hate any
Having been the soul author
With the strength I had
I could have built and fortified a mansion
But today the evil boomerang

Still Brothers

Born of a poor rural woman
We shared her pain and trouble
But survived to date
When the worst struck
We felt it both
When neighbours shouted
She protected both
We were brothers then
We were, when we grew up Valentine
We had a oneness
We had an understanding
You would say not that Valerie…!!
I would never argue you'll remember
And we grew to be men
Like branches we are now
One stretching to the North
The other to the South
But share a common root
Then why not it be so
That we be still Valerie and Valentine
As at four
Why would you propagate a time bomb?
Why would you have reason against a brother
Would you devote reconciliation?
Why will you wish me the dead?
Why will you not look back?
Why will you discard Moreblessing's teachings?
Do you remember at eight?
Do you remember us around her?
We were brothers then

And we would share all
But my sight you'll not stand
Just but for material gains and power
But will that ever remedy the family ills
My brother, unity alone
No matter how badly you feel today
We are still brothers, my brother
Let us unite as brothers
Let us think positively as brothers
And forever we'll be stars my brothe

Life Changes

Miserably brought up he was
With no love in sight from day old
But through tough times there he stands today
Comfort was mere classroom talk
And never known to him through his childhood
But to heights he is now
Pain was the best language he understood
Used and abused yesterday he was
Protection was not known to him
Except his of fields in green
But through such evil he stands tall today
He stands firm and flanked by lieutenants
A dream that came true

Tunes From Yesterday

Saddening and disheartening it was
Like a cyclone it is now
Once strong but crumbled today
The marks of history will tell

My poor heart had love
Love that grew from an almost wilting seed
Least expecting monsters abreast
And my sword under the pillow

Like the hurricane times, have moved fast
Leaving me no time to understand
Even if odds would be against me
My heart is tormented, torn and in tatters

Yes, at times, times most
Tunes from yesterday echo
But irredeemable the situation is now
I gave a monster heart

I trusted and went head over heals
The worse any man can do
Doing right, thought I was
And today painfully, thorns I harvest

I regret wholly, sadly and endlessly
But to my prejudice tunes from yesterday
Are fast fading painfully
But happy she is with my neighbour

A heart that loved once
When insensitively broken, breaks
Mine is yet without deceit loved
But a harvest of thorns it has been now

Decision When It Matters

Brave and bold at times we've to become
Critical and strong at times we've to be
Considerate and forgiving at time we've to be
But at dusk when it matters,
decisions have to be solidly taken

Decisions may be painful and thorny pricking to take
Decisions may be difficult to craft and pass
Decisions may invite pain, loneliness and confusion
But when it matters
No matter the gravity spelt
Decisions may imperatively have to be taken

Sorrowful you may remain
Disheartened you may feel
Disturbed entirely you may remain
But when it matters
Decisions are inevitable

Dead Silence

When the silence pierces through all nerves
Memories recall things past
But comfort fades and distances
As reality burdens the heart.
Inviting tears to stream down.
Sorrow gravely dominate
And friendly echoes distantly wail with no comfort,
meaning and assurance
Thus causing untold pain to descend

Looking at yesterday in day light
The roses were fresh and shining
With an inviting aroma sent
But today all bow in mourning
For the gust turn of events

Least when the blow was anticipated
A bullet straight, accurate and sharp,
In the so open ground with no foliage
Was discharged to harm and make history

Yes, history was heralded
And scaring is the unknown today
The unknown disturbs and scares
The unknown eat the heart and wearies the body
But on regaining momentum
Redress, fortify and keep agoing

Lovely smiles, hugs yes they come
And leaving you with tears they do equally

For not many are true
Remember unmistakenly and unfooled
Boldness and consciousness will keep you unbroken
For once broken
The fragments amalgamate not soon

Marks Of Yesterday

Yes the scales of the skin cover the delicate heart
The scales assure and ensure total warmth
The warmth that gives the courage to sacrifice
The sacrifice to stand aloft and
Giving praises to the beaming rose
The rose with petals bright and full of life
Such life still tender
Such life of a juvenile, agile and principled
The agility that gives hope of the fresh breeze
And anchor the principles already prevalent
Thus a new life unveils
A life that overshadows all the ills of yesterday
Such ills that left marks, memories and a sense of volition

Not All Dreams

One morning in summer
As the sun was in its western descend
She looked hopefully in the north
And was wholly woed
She consented in serene
And changed the course of travel
The pasture was attractively green
All fields had life and in green
Jacarandas blooming and attracting
The hibiscus showing their tender red petals
And lavendas sending a distinct scent
Inviting, breath taking and pleasant

She looked to the South at noon
Compared the lives and contrasted
Nothing caught her eye and she looked down
The desert was hot and barely supporting life
All trees with ceased translocation and loosing leaf
And the oasis drying up making it impossible to survive
Life would not be possible

Once again she looked to the North
Grave audience to her instincts
Questioned her motive
But the sixth sense had crawled in

She gave back to the South
With smiles and dreams
Dreams of a splendid life
But all that glitters…

Not many realise

Not long drought came to the North
And life disappeared
Tears rolled down
Realising the oasis
Still had life
While she in shumbles
In morning and disarray

Sour Relations

Thought the bond inseparable and entrusted
But missiles pierce my flesh today in broad day light

When I look to the marks of history
I squat and make prayers
Prayers for redemption and sufficiency of grace

When I revisit my time track
I regret and make curses
I had not fore seen such life ills and attendant consequences

Human mind as I understand today
A thought distant yesterday
Can change and deceive

But as I head for the galoes
I stop to say, had I known
And in the next world after resurrection
I will be conscious
For once beaten twice shy

No Love Under The Sun

I have wholly loved and given myself before
I have heartily trusted, embraced and believed before
I have given total hope, dreams and bowed before
But in the twitch of an eye at dawn
Like a volcano erupting
All my efforts had no place
No one would ever recall or remember
Remembering would unveil the evils of mankind
Remembering would manifest weevils boring
And the termites sucking sap
From the love stem anchored in the oasis
As the cultivated facets are trans located from the roots
It pains and eats the heart day and night
It disturbs and worries the heart all the time
It thwarts the rising newly born love in its infancy
How cruel other species can become

There is no love under the sun
Such love the world cherishes
Such love all life anticipates
There is no true and everlasting love under the sun
Those who had love were derailed and discouraged
Those whose hearts had love were betrayed and buried thus
no one will love today

I had loved truly and honestly
But I won't now
I had trusted without deceit and reservations
But I won't now
I had dreamed and would fight till emancipation

But I won't now.

I had believed and accommodated with all my heart
But I won't now
They pushed me to a far end to regain my stance
They had no heart, no feelings, no…
They were thoughtless, ruthless, and…
They had disregard of my rights and I was exasperated,
But I still would bitterly swallow the bitter pill

I have been a victim provoking sympathy
But I will be strong now
I have been made to pay for what I did not owe
But I will be strong now
I have been made to crawl when I should have walked
Made to stand when I should have sat
Made to run when I should have flew
But I will be resentful and more careful now
I will be a man now
A true man with lion prowess
Thus keep my head above the tide

There is no love under the sun
The radiated rays sublimed all the residue
Thus pain, distrust hate and hurt will prevail
Such prevalence that will kill the world
The world needs love and peace to live
The love that has no limitations and bounds
The love that crosses boundaries and borders

Rolling Turmoil

What I heard was bitter
     to absorb
What I read was hard
     to believe
What I saw was thorny
     to imagine
But I had to be a man
A man with a vice grip
Such grip as to uphold my principles
I had to be bold
And I would

Hard I tried but my heart sunk
To the limit I had been taken
To breaking point I had been stretched
And like the falling winter leaves
The tamper exploded in all dimensions and directions

All like a big joke as we talked it started
But to marrow and through the effect went
Ravaging the joyous mood upon arrival
But such is normal and a part of life

Like two dogs in a fight for bone
A dead lock was reached
None of us would melt and become the weaker
For fear of being thought the villain

Who would carry blame remained shadowed
Who had instigated and propelled the trouble was unknown

Who had the remedy to the malady was not known
And for how long would it perch
And continue to cause turmoil
Such rolling turmoil that never cease

Love For A Friend

To love is to do the best for him
With no eyes for anything in return
To love is to be selfless
And have beast foolery buried
Buying at no price the heart of a friend
And make him the prince of your heart
And vow never to hurt
And take it upon yourself to hate all ill winds
Thus guard jealously your goard of love
Given to you by your God at no price
And your prize to love would be abundant life
That when you abuse you would fall head ward
And the test you would have drastically failed
Such drama imminent in our life today

If My Heart Could Tell

Blind like a pregnant bat you are
Though you cover great distance in fight
A lot misses your eye
Which explains the trend of situations
Your stance is never easy to tell
Great better bat characteristic then
Are you an animal or bird,
For animals cannot fly but you can
For birds do not have little ones sucking but you do
So what is your real identity?
Where do you really stand?

My heart is in untold pain
Great pain that ruptures all efforts
To forge strides ahead
And disturbs the serenity of the heart
My heart cannot tell were you stand
And I wish I knew…
I wish I could tell…
I wish I could understand…
I wish I could believe…
I cherish I could see all that transpires
Behind the iron curtain
Such discoveries would consolidate
My expectations for a beaming rose

If my heart could tell
Pain would be distant
Worry would be history
Stress would live no mark;

Marks that trigger hate
Such hate that invites revenge
Blood revenge that heals no world
For the world needs peace
The raw peace in its delicacy

If my heart could tell
Life would be joyous
For I would ever be on guard
If my heart could tell
I would sing from the mountain top
I would fight all wars
I would break all bounds
I would harmonise the war pendulum
But my heart has limitations

If my heart could tell
I would squat and pray
Prayers for a perpetual unison
Prayers for total peace and harmony
Prayers for love and rain
Prayers for…
Yes prayers for everything

If my heart could tell
I would subscribe to the devotion
That makes an important part of me
Such part which when trampled on
Shatters and never amalgamate
If my poor heart could tell
I would tell myself to be strong
Such strength that urges strides uphill

Good Bye Maka!!

With all my heart I loved
Would you object Maka…!
Would you say you never realised
Would you say that was not good enough?
Would you Maka…!!

With all zeal I had worked
For the blossoming rose to keep shining
Sweat oozed as I fought
Calories dripped as I struggled
But never would I give up
Never would I surrender
Would you say all this you never realised?
And never would I give up

With the meagre calories in the reserves
I tried to erect a fortress
Such a fortress to protect the mansion.
And took joy in the distance covered
But short lived it was and today I mourn

I had given up everything for you
I had fought for you
I had believed you
I had…yes I had
But when push comes to shove
The blame is put on me
But Maka… am I to blame?
Am I Maka…!

If I am, let us successfully part then
Let our paths run parallel and distant
Let us never meet again
For my heart has just learnt to, let go
But I still will wish you joy and uncontaminated blessings

Retain Your Colours

They may not believe
When you explain
They may doubt your
Credentials and mettle
They may push you aside
Or trod over you
But always look upon
Your principles, ways and values
Always remain the real person in you
No matter how they treat you
Always retain your virtues and never pervert

To the limit you may be taken
To the worst end you may be stretched
But two wrongs make no right
Thus remain well valued and mannered
They may prick your eye
They may trickle your conscience
And expect you to go loose
They may manhandle you
And expect you to crumble and thus compromise
They may really take advantage of you
But always retain your colours
The colours that make you the person you are
The person who's a model to many
Such a model that inspires the world
The inspiration that conquers

Tormented Soul

As I listened to my poor tormented heart
A multitude unanswered questions sprouted
And like the stone wall of Berlin
All my confidence crumbled to nuclear dust
I tried to rise and keep balance on my feet
I tried to pick some comfort from the serenity of the night
I tried to console my tattered soul
But tears as in a butchered bull,
Gashed painfully leaving heightened sorrowful marks

My heart welcomed and accommodated
Wholly and truly
But a monster had been given heart
And today on I will never look back

In Milly, the heart thought a friend had come
In Milly, the heart thought the gap left by
The late mother was now filled
But never was that to be
Instead it was a harvest of thorns
Instead I would be jeered at
I would be a laughing stock
I had trusted soon and went head over heels
I had prematurely passionately kissed
And had even made love
Never will I be fooled this much and far
Never will I embrace a woman again

Milly broke my heart and cause
In the night I thought I needed

The warmth of her body
In the night I thought I needed
That lovely whisper into my ear
In the night I thought I cherished
The warm and tender caress
But there in the cold I was
And I will never give up my fragile heart again

As you wished today
We will part ways indefinitely
Let the parting be successful
Let us never meet again
For the wounds would never heal

As you enjoy without my persistent
Bother, harassment and inconvenience
I wish you total joy and happiness
I wish you uncontaminated blessings
And let all your childhood wishes unveil
In the manner you've always dreamt

Let the wishes unveil in the
Manner that forever will see your happiness
For I've always loved your happiness too
I will always wish you happiness that is endless

As they take over from what I failed to possess
As they take the reigns I failed to own
As they grab wholly what I failed to manipulate
I only stop to wish them all that gives them credit to prevail
I wish them life and all that comes with it.

Goat Sure Footed

Never will take to be foot trodden
For goat sure-footed I am
And will swim upstream amid dolphins
But maintain the head above the tide

Never will I succumb to what the heart despises for that is
not the anatomy making me up
I will continue to be esteemed and persevere
I will never pervert
I will never walk down hill with no grip on the foot
I will trust no stranger at dusk and dawn
I will be conscious all times even in my dream
For the world now is flooded with ills

Never will my heart take pretence
Never will my ways and virtues be derailed
Never will I break to what I don't subscribe to
But will thrive to remain me at all times

Our Neighbours

Neighbours may be friends
Such friends we need at times
The friends showing up with advise at times
Friends telling you his pastime when you are not home
Friends telling you who comes when you're left
Friends telling you who comes home even at night
Neighbours may thus be friends
Such friends with shades of love, hate and jealous
Such friends with deceitful and cheerful spells

Our neighbours always keep an eye on us
They always keep trek of all our events and scenes
They always remain informed of our progress and failures
Neighbours always keep abreast with all we do
They may formerly never be in our home
But know all that exist in our home
All that is planned in our home
Our neighbours know us well to even destroy us

Our neighbours are friends who may avoid us
But pass detailed researches regarding us
To their neighbours and friends
They may never smile when they look at us
But remain informed of what steps we are taking
Our neighbours are good observers and researchers
Thus I've learnt to seclude neighbours in my circle
The circle I treasure so well
Thus avoid hurt when they trumpet ills
Neighbours forever I will avoid
For their winds blow thorns

Neighbours, neighbours…!
Where do you stand, my neighbours?

The Tested Love

In the whole universe and beyond
Definitions have been spelt and pronounced
Theories propounded and passed
Explanations offered and welcomed
But nothing exists in blue print for adoption
Nothing exists as the sole principle and guide

The tested love lies in the individual heart
It does not come in a day
But graduates from a lot of testing
In love comes test of trust
And many are seen to be hypocrites
In love there is test of honest
And many show signs of greedy
In love there are numerous tests
And such tests prove love
The love that lives
The love that has meaning
And u fruit
Such fruit sweet and true
Such love that knows no hate
Such love that sees no failures
Such love that cheers when all jeer
Such love that you need
Such love I need also
The kind of love true
The kind of love raw and uncorrupted
The kind of love untapped yet ripe
The kind of love real
Yes true tested love is hard to come by

Wishful Heart

As I sit in the breath taking sun
I watch pedestrian volumes crisscrossing
All in terrific moods as though
All is well in their hearts
I hate myself to think I'm
The only failure
As I look to the East to see
The blooming jacarandas captivating
I take comfort in the November breeze
That brings some absorbing relief

My memories recapture the evils
Of mankind when night falls
I worry and think of possible remedies
Hard I try to work out a plan
That would in the long run present
An everlasting remedy
I try even harder with each passing day
But when the blows of night
Pounce on the weak
I feel the pain slowly engulf my patience
I feel an upsurge of anger
I feel the urge to protect the vulnerable
But the ammunition betrays me
And with no one to listen
I shift my transfixed eyes and
Contemplation to the chanting weaver birds
As they fly up and sing sweet melodies
My heart is woed and I wish
I could fly and join them

A Day In Africa Unit Square

I see people of all races
I see people of all strengths and weaknesses
I see people full of pathos
I see people I envy
In the square you can see all personalities

Some come running and pass
Some come strolling and have
Brief moments of stay at various corners
Some come in pairs
While others as individuals

Some come with joy beaming faces
Some come with triumphatic faces
Some come with faces written trouble and suffering
In the square you can see all personalities

Vendors get to all corners
Wary though of the consequences
Muggers patrol the peripheral zones
But hearts thumping in fear
As the visitor appreciate the colourful jacarandas
As the visitor takes a look at the water points
I only praise the unnoticed officer at work
Who makes it a better place
Who makes peace herald and telecast
But his efforts receiving no notice
As though he does not exist

My Love

Words and phrases are under statements
And never will explain my love
Never will say how true I am
My poor heart will love,
My poor heart will be true
Such truth that bears fruit
The fruits that creates a fort
The fort that deters all evil whirlwinds

Yes I've said it before, but surely not in this manner
And the winter memories will stay
The memories that brought a new era
An era with total transformation
Such transformation that enhances the base
The base the heart will bank on

If you should lend me your ears
Trumpets I'll blow above hills and mountains
I'll sing my beautiful songs
The songs that praise the person you are
You rare personality

Like an almost wilting seed in winter
It all seemed in the beginning
Watered timely and continuously has seen it grow
Such growth instilling the utmost hope
The hope that shimmers like a blooming rose

With dainties we hike now
With oneness we embrace today

We share all
We see no boundaries
We are now truly in love

Let us today even give it our best
Let the lapse of time see no lapse of the relationship
Let the dreams graduate into reality
And our joys and aspirations live to expectations

Let no colossial forces stray your thoughts
Let no man prostitute your mind
Let no one poison the person I've known you to be

With all my heart I love you
The love from the gorge of my poor heart
A heart that was wholly captivated
A heart that will want to rest now
And will not embrace any ills

With all my heart I'll love
With all my love, ill love you
And love honestly, persistently
Such honest that sees no deceit

Choices

When the heart is faced with choices
Remarkably reduce the tickle on the heart
Make an unshaken total focus on the life retina
Shut all other steel screens
Keep your head up
Close your eyes and clench a first
Tighten the fist and stance
Open your eyes and clench a fist
Tighten the fist and stance
Open your eyes and look down
Stretch your ear and pick the first whisper
Look to the South
To pick the first vision
Approaching in an immaculate gown and crown
Embrace and turn to the north
Look back and you fall
Look up and visions of prosperity unveil

Decisions crack hearts from the core
And spell joy, pain
Thus pensively listen to the heart
Give it proper audience
Rid haste conclusions
Ample time to investigate pays
Damages are never repairable
For repairs are never total
Choices are not easy to make

If a choice is to be made
Put your mind to it,

Turn 360 degrees
Explore all possibilities
While your eyes are focused on the vision
Be conscious of sweeping winds of deceipt
Think through choices,
Consult widely and honestly
Be sober at all time
Keep your head above the tide
And settled for the best choice

My son, my little David

When you're full of energy my son
Get yourself together and realise your cause
Look up and brace up
Make your shoulders square
And amble with ears alert
Get to the most height
Pull your sword my son
But keep in hiding till they assail.

My son, my little David
Look up and receive your blessing
Look up and receive your power

You are my child
You are my blood
And you will not perish

With all the power and energy
Confront your enemy unshaking
Look straight into his eye
And keep advancing

My son, my little David
With your energy you will conquer
You will conquer even beyond

My son, my little David
Believe in yourself in all seasons
It requires strategy and faith to win
And your wars will not trouble you

Sweeter Than Honey

Your love is sweeter than honey
Raw honey from nectar
Your love is deeper than all ponds
Such depth that gives me comfort
Your love is real and passionately true
Such truthfulness that commands sacrifice

Your smile like the heavenly stars
Gives me joy and assurance
Your love like a tap root
Has gone deeper than the hurricane can destroy
The look in your eye is so assuring and wholly captivating
The assurance that tells the heart to do only good

I love you, Darlin'
Such love I have never felt before
I will be commited today, Darlin'
Such commitment I have not known before
I will settle now. Darlin'
A thought distant yesterday
You have proved to be all I need
With virtually nothing to boast with but a heart

A heart to capacity full of love
I will love you till the end of time

No other woman will draw any nearer, now
No other woman has ever taken me so deep and far
No other woman has ever been so natural and mannered
No other woman will ever steal my heart again

I will kiss no other woman again
I will use the word love to no other, again
I will not ask any other to undress before me
I will never give reason to hurt you

You stole my heart truly
The whole of my heart
And my love is growing by day
I will give you the best
Such best from a heart innocent and truthful
Such best you have not known
Such best that comes with the unique tenderness in me

I love you, Darlin'
The kind of love real and tested
The kind of love richer than gold
The kind of love heavier than lead
The kind of love stronger than any soldier regiment on the
war front
The kind of love solid and harder than solidified magma
The love deeper and fresher than the Mississipi waters
The love even denser than the Equatorial forest
The love you will know to be unique

You captured my poor heart
And promised to love honestly
Such love I have searched for in years
Years that were so full of pain
Years that were so full of sin
Years that I will not want to remember
For the memories tear the heart
The heart that is delicate and fragile

Jilted, abused and robbed I was
But thought myself in love then
Embraced, kissed and sexed I was
And believed in love I was
But lend me your ears today
As I blow my trumpet to unveil the black past
I had not known love then
And only wish I knew

What I saw was not love
What I felt was not love
What I lived in and believed to be love was not
For love sees no pain, trouble and pretences
Real love comes with sacrifice
Sacrificing all for the other and standing with the other at
all times

I am dirty, bewildered and agonised, Darlin'
I am not as I wish I should have been
I should have waited for you
But they as though with love
Helped me into that n^{th} deep mangy pool of pain and sin
I feel empty and worthless today
I feel abused, drained and destroyed today
But help me build again and bury the black past
I cry endlessly today
But let us purposefully start a new
Let us now start right and firmly

Hopeful Hearts

When the hearts unveil purposefulness
Draw closer with each day
Make unshaking plans
And fight with no turn backs

When the hearts understand the set goals
Give the relationship the best
Like a farmer watering his seed
Give the equal care to the relationship

When the hearts focus on the same objective
Work purposefully, tirelessly and leave no stone unturned
Deny yourself sleep and work till the break of day
With everything invested into it, the stars will forever shine

When you welcome and open up for one another
Pick and learn what pleases the other
Appreciate and respect the other fully
And in so doing you'll get to heights

When both hearts sacrifice
Nothing will derail progressive plans
Nothing will bring pain and mistrust
And the awaited tomorrow will be beaming

When one heart lags
The oscillations will treble
The dreams and aspirations will be offset
And a common purpose will be distant

When the hearts grow in love
No whirlwinds will destroy the plans
No ill winds will impair your vision
And together you will conquer all wars

When the hearts embrace with unified commitment
All blessings will descend from the heavens
All dreams will transform into reality
And smiles will perpetuate

Broken Heart

How many times does it have to be ?
How many times do I have to feel the painful blows?
How many times do I have to spend sleepless nights in morning?
How many times do I have to hear your apologies?
Apologies that are not
Apologies now repeated as song
How many times…? How many…?

I am human and tire
For to breaking point you have drawn my patience
You have stretched my patience too far
You have proved we can no longer embrace
You have shown me well how bad I am
I have seen it fit to concur with your thoughts
I have been convinced it cannot be for convenience
Not for convenience and it never can, never will

Why did you leave me plan to such heights and meaning?
Why did you encourage strides of such magnitude?
Why did you make me broaden my wishes and intentions?
Why did you leave me look at matters of such dimensions
Anyway it was your concealed plan
And actions echo louder than words
Actions communicate well to those with eyes open

You have my wishes when the day breaks
Just like any who has come, briefly stayed and left
When we meet again why not embrace
Why not talk like we never had problems

Why not still share the same advice
Why not still exchange the same smiles

It had to be today
And let it be
As long it pleases your heart
Though mine is broken

Sacrifice

When you journey into the unknown
When in the land unfamiliar you dine with strangers
When you turn your back to the comfort of your home
That will be a sacrifice my son

When you sweat in such remote land
When you forgo even your sleep
And stretch your brains to the limit
I will call you a man my son

When you fight to give them a name
When your resources converge for their cause
And you put your mind together for the single minded goal
I will call you my hero my son

When you become the true ambassador of the family
When you earn our name credit and respect
And let showers of praise descend
Then my hero you'll always be

When you remain the torch bearer
When you live by example
And make all emulate and implement
Then you'll always have my respect dear son

My son, always unveil that heart of flesh
Such heart I've always talked of
Such heart unique and heals the world
With this heart my son, you'll be hero to all

You will be a hero to all my son
For it takes nothing but selflessness
It takes a heart boast-less
It takes a heart not egocentric

You will be my hero my son
If from up the ladder you remember us
If the fruits of your strides we share
If our oneness remains firmly unshaken through all tests

My little son, my only son
Yes the sole mark of my biological potency
My blood, my hope, my pillar
You are everything to me son
Thus make that sacrifice
For you are the sacrifice
Sacrifice son, sacrifice your life
Without sacrifices your will be empty
Not only, but worthless, pathetic and directionless
Sacrifice your life my son, my dear son

Among The Tonga

As I looked into the Zambezi waters
The challenge grew tenfold and over
And from the core of the heart answers unveiled
The Binga unfriendly weather planted seeds of
perseverance
And the Tonga abreast encouraged
He even wish me, well on my journey back
'marumba kaboto he said
And his smile gave me comfort"

As the mosquitoes cruelly invaded my little dagga hut
I cursed the spirit of misery, poverty dominating my life
front
But the Tonga abreast, Chiboto encouraged
He would squeeze my hand, a gesture I knew
I had a vision among the Tonga
And would not come home to roast
Till my dreams had transformed into reality

When there was no joy at the harbour my heart sunk
But among the Tonga it was normal
I would never look back
For the inertia was gone and soon I would get to heights
Rock hard as it was I would never surrender
For among the Tonga you learn of strange, pathetic and
unbelievable scenarios

As I saw the shaking and almost sinking fishermen
I would fear for them
But among the Tonga the worst has happened

Among the Tonga, hippos have sunk canoes
Among the Tonga are orphans cursing the waters
But soon I was to learn to face any tide
I was to be strong and never easily give up
I would never rest till what I desired was realised

Among the Tonga are legendary stories I treasured
For the Tongas are a people with a history of togetherness
A People with the same fighting spirit and resolve
And history has it, dating back to late 50's

When I heard the hippos communicating in their language
And the determined fishermen went past
A new heart was born
I never would easily give up
For among the Tonga you learn to be strong

When I heard the elephants descending to the waters
I feared for his attack
But among the Tonga it is not scaring
And when morning came with droppings on the yard
I perspired terribly learning the elephant was responsible
Among the Tonga it is nothing to worry about
Thus a relief descended learning I was no longer in danger
He was gone and would return well into the night
As he went for a bath

When buffaloes bellowed I tightly squeezed the Tonga
abreast
But among the Tonga such noise are normal
Such noises are no threat

Poverty Dark Cloud

It is all untold misery in my home
A home with my sweat I've tried to build
But wholly submerged in pain and tears
Tears that may never dry

Cries are breaking through roofs of my falling hut
And my children like starved plants are dying painfully
But I do care
Maybe it is my fate
Rest in peace my children

I have desperately tried through all seasons
But not even an inch have the biting events turned
I have done the best in my energy
And my heart tells me so
My situation has remained shadowed
And I will worry to my death bed

Hard I have tried all my life
with my days starting earlier than dawn
Sweat has oozed like torrentials
But no answers have descended forth

The pain has cut through all my nerves
And I no longer have an iota to stand the pressure
My memory and will power is now ruptured
I am discouraged
And may never rise again

Day and night I have tried
But no answers have come
No shades of light have shown
No shades of hope have been reradiated
To resurrect the dumped spirit
My days have remained black, blank and painful
Comfort remains unknown to me
And to my death slowly I will walk
Painful it will be
With nothing in my hand
Except cracks of poverty

Seasons as though in a race
Have gone by faster than lightning
But answers have remained distant
For I have groaned and never gained
Failed but never falsified
I have fallen but never fooled
Poverty by day has grown
But I never gambled
With eyes full of pathos
They have looked into my path helplessly
But as though the rains will descend
The dark cloud has grown
Leaving the little warmth blown

Determined though at dusk in my black gown,
I gave chase and would never frown
But make positive marked strides
And never allow the evil total victory
For pricking my conscience
I would insert the spike

And turn the spindle
Thus alleviate the poverty

Poverty ravages the serenity in homes
And wailing in my home cannot go unabated
Resilience and persistence are facets I have learnt
I will fight with all tooth and nails
I will never give up till
A change I witness
Determination and will power drive motives
And it is not in me to throw in the towel
I will be resolute, stand
And fight for a change in my life

Tribute To The Late Athletes

In a bid to raise our flag high
Your hopes could not be higher
Than you thought
In a show you were determined
What they thought you excel, the drama ended prematurely
The show was never to be
Rest in peace

You were a marvel to watch
But your watch ran too fast
To end your circle
When a lot we still expected
From your strides so unique
Rest in peace
Our hearts profusely bleed today
As we look back in time
But only to see memories
And accept you'll never descend
Rest in peace

Where ever your souls are
Let nothing sail there to disturb your peace
And destroy your rest
And subject, you to unnecessary pressures
Rest in peace

Days will come and go
Seasons interchange
But things will never be the same on the track
This gap will forever perpetuate

You are irreplacable
Rest in peace

Death

A necessity which cripples when it does
Living us mute and disturbed
Fear and disbelief hovering
As the memory of yesterday deepens
And sending turmoil and puzzles now
All like a dream we buy the pain
The itching pain of loss

We glare up sorrowfully
We gaze on what used to be his best seat
With pain doubt is cast off
All bridging across the denial stage
Tears flowing like the deep waters of the Mississipi

As though awaiting an answer, we squat serenely
The pain of loss cutting through all nerves
As memories of his jokes show up again
But his soul already in another world
A world we wish for
Though we all hate to die

All converge to console and comfort
Flowers shower in
Condolences fall from all directions
As they look back in time
When he was a prominent and shimmering figure
But peacefully lying in a hardwood box now
A box no man would want
A box that evidence a frisk to the other world
A world believed peaceful and harmonious

Recalling his works and ways
All hearts sink in agony,
As the mind tries to recall yesterday
With all those smiles and jokes.
The soul is tormented
But death is a necessary end which comes when it does

No power can deviate the death call
No life force can deflect his sword
Big or small feel this blow
Rich or poor there is no exception
Ugly or beautiful all taste the bitter fate
Like a wind he assails from all ends
Even when life is sweetest
Even when one is out for a honey moon

Death is never satisfied
Gallant leaders come and go
Progressive minds come and go
Rogue elements come and go
Intelligent scientist come and go
Death takes all in a row
No one is immune to death
All life is mortal

Gallant Fighter

Your voice still echo
Sending a stimuli to review your works
The works commendable and remembered
Your name will stay vivid
Your works forever will be remembered
Your works forever will be appreciated
Though earth has now cruelly engulfed you

In you was a fighter
A fighter who realised his cause
Thus excelled patriotically
Today our praises and thanks to you
Rest in peace colleague

The pain of your death will remain fresh
For you left a gap
Such a gap that will perpetuate
You are irreplaceable colleague
You had a unique personality
With patriotic principles at the front
Rest in peace

We fly our flags today
Enjoying the fruits you fought for
But we never cease to praise and honour you
Your lion prowess brought us independence
Your love for the people brought us freedom
Forever your name will live comrade
In spite of all hardship comrade
Your sole goal remained at heart

The goal to emancipate your people
The goal to untangle the bondage enslaving them
Our love for you will stay comrade

In you was a true man
A man for the people
A benefactor with all love
Who fought with all zeal
Determined for the single minded goal
To bring freedom to fellow men
Thus free Zimbabwe
Rest in peace

From My Heart My Song

The summer downpours come and pass
Jacarandas bloom and lose leaf
Winter winds blow and go
Spring springs aboard briefly stays and leave again

As I busk, I contemplate
At the core of my mind I weigh
All day I ponder
But meagre I sieve
On the core of my heart lies the chapter
The lines communicating it all

The birds melodiously sing
And like light showers the songs permeate
Making all meaning I treasure
Whispering to myself becomes inevitable
Time still rolls by
But one thing still remains the same

Peacefully flowing deep waters,
Steal my admiration momentarily
Regaining my conscious mind
I give praises and thanks
As the trees and grasses respectfully sway
I stop to think but…

The memory of yesterday disturbs me
At extreme moments, thundery blowing me
Regaining my stance I walk briskly ahead
Reproaching and comforting though

What a paradox
But tomorrow still stands shimmering

Calling all patience
I rise and firmly stand
I fight for a tomorrow
A tomorrow to give me a name
A name that will stay

When all seems dull and collapsing
When my world appears doomed
I cease to worry
For worry does nothing but harm more
Worry disturbs and hurts
But determined for that day I rise

Time tickles fast
But in my heart emanates no word
Conscience tells me a day awaits
For all await the moment
The moment to unveil it all
The revelation that will tell it all

Make A Difference

In your youthful days is the moment
The ripe moment if focused
The moment when you are full of energy
The moment when you are in the right frame
This is the time for you, to make a difference
A difference in your life
A big difference
A vast difference
A notable and remarkable difference

Make a difference
In the life drama in which you are a player
A player sometimes playing a sorrowful role
Be vibrant, dynamic and conscious
Be focused and follow the vision
Yes, even when uncertain is the environment
Yes, even when volatile is the situation
Yes, even when the terrain is uneven, at times rough

During your youthful days, spent time
Productively, jealously and qualitatively
During your youthful days avoid rushed decisions
influenced decisions
Take time, take your time
Yes and make informed decisions
Produce and store in your granaries
Enough to sustain life
Forget a while about reproducing
Instead, think of making a difference
Yes a notable difference this season

Devote your time in total
Commit your resources in total
Dedicate your heart not in parts
Devote your time to personal growth and development
Seek knowledge, for it is power
Be conscious of the world around you
Be positive and live not to regret

My Loving Heart

The bitter waters tear and wear my cheeks
As I see the gradual waste of time
And the feeling of loss flood my mind
Poisoning my rest and peace
But I never cease to cast hope

with hope I still watch sunrise and sunset
I still rise to see seasons interchanging.
And birth and death alternating
But still optimistic for smiles
Though at times I feel humiliated and worn out

With my youth wearing away
Falling into bits like a cloth long hung in the sun
My worries prick my nerves
Realising the world does not wait for me
I rid my pessimism
Though ashamed of my weakness

When I feel grief
Which is most often?
I go out and seek companions in the trees
I listen to melodious songs from the hustle dare
I find pleasure in the moon and stars speak to me
Thus console and bring me to life again

Night falls and in my thoughts comes torture
By morning the darkness has swallowed all good
Living me bewildered and puzzled
And all I say is, why, why and why?

A Song For Mama

In jubilation I jump sky high
In the rain, in the cold and all times
Appreciating the role, your critical role
Unparalleled role performed by you mama

You are a star mama, my mother
A shining star that leads the way
And you have always been
On this special day mama
I will sing a song
My beautiful song dedicated to a mother
A mother from whose womb I'm a product
A song to pronounce how special you are
How important you are Mama'
How beautiful...
How hardworking and innovative
You are enterprising and creative Mama

You are assidious Mama
You have always...
And my heart salutes you
You are my hero Mama
And may the Lord, the good Lord
Richly bless you
Yes, with many days
Days full of love
Days full of all that your heart cherishes
Let the Lord wipe all your tears Mama

Your love Mama is immeasurable,
The burden you carried was too big
It was in every respect
At times I saw it, but was too young to acknowledge
I could see it mama
Yes, I could
Which is why I say
I would never repay
Even if I had to
The price would be too high.
A lot for your son, you did
It cannot all be counted
It cannot all be measured
Yet evidence is everywhere mama
Be blessed with many days
Many days is my prayer for you
Yes for you mama
This will be my song mama
My song confessing
That I would never repay
Be blessed mama. My mother

When I Marry

Indeed, it is a fact of life for all creation,
All males and indeed all
Mammals, reptiles, birds, alike need partners
Man is no exception: men need wives too
The reasons for marrying are diverse though
Yes, each man has own reasons

I will increase production power when I marry
My wife and children will till the land
The more I have, the more power
The land they will till
The flock they will tend
Yet I will decide how much to sell and when
I will be ultimate: the final authority in the home

I will have sex when I want it
Yes, even three times a day as with paracetamol
That will not be negotiated, in rain, thunder or lightning
My wife will never own and never share,
My assets
She will be, my tool too
Just like any of my other tools in the home

Everything in the home shall be mine
Indeed everything including her whole being
The children she will not own too
They will be called my name and no other
She will be called my name and no other
And I will decide on all sexuality

Why I Want To Marry

I vividly recall as a young girl
I would dream and wish
One day I would marry
But did I understand what it all meant…

Stories were told
Books were read
Marriages were seen
But why, would I marry?

The obvious would be reproduction
Having off springs of my own, my own boys and girls
I would be called mama
How much I cherished that, ooh!
Little did I know reproduction demanded production
The little boys and girls would need to eat
Food in the morning, afternoon and before bed time

I would decide on my husband's income
It would be ours
I would be consulted by her people on family issues
Our problems would be collectively owned
I would decide what to wear, eat and when to sleep
That would be independence and freedom that
Comes with marriage
I would marry… I would marry...

I would always be in his warm arms
I would always have that tender caress
That kiss, touch

I would have my own home, my own yard,
My own garden, flowers, I would...

I would cook for him, the best dishes
Help him dress and convince him he's like no other
And that for him I'll would always wait
Upon him I would always wait- I would love
For to love was to commit myself
In marrying I was looking for a friend
My eyes would go no further
That's why I married him

Life

Yes this is my question today
This is my question to you all
What is the point? What is the use?
For life is full of pain, tears, harshness
Life is full of struggles, sadness, tragedies
Yes, is full of heart breaking moments
Moments like the loss of a beloved one
Loss of a beloved friend
Loss of a beloved… yes a beloved one.

In this life realise, and acknowledge colleagues
Yes that life is too short to learn from your own
Mistakes alone,
Look up, square up, brace up and awaken
Realise a candle loses nothing by lighting another
From Fari's loss claim a giant and positive step
Be enlightened, be motivated to realise purposefulness in
life
Think like a champion
A champion does not always go where there is a way but
where there is no way but leave a trail, a mark, for years will
shimmer and declare: once
A champion was here
A champion in the frame of Fari, the poet
The artist, a force to reckon

This life…! our life ends,
At times soon, at times late
And no man immune to this,

It is hidden and no man will know

No man has ever known

Oh… oooh!
My heart bleeds at the loss
But celebrates the lesson learnt,
Fari died not in vain
As witnessed by multitudes that converged
Multitudes from far and wide
Multitude from across society

As we laid you to rest
Tears rolled down
It was such a sombre mood
Realising this was your last lap
Your chapter had ended

The Right Seed

Be warned…
Be watchful…
Be witful…
For the devil's word is a counter seed,
A seed that seeks to undo, to uproot
Surely what God's word planted

God's word is the real seed
Consume in abundance the word
To create a fortress that shakes not
A fortress never to be conquered

Be sure to possess the right seed
In adversity, turn to God
Turn to God through all seasons

Time To Sacrifice All

This is the time to sacrifice all
This is the time and no time later
With the best of our abilities, wilfully
Sacrifice all and inherit the Kingdom
Let us commit ourselves fully for the single minded goal
       to inherit the Kingdom
       to inherit the promises
For this cannot be the moment for the devil
Let us not side step to give the devil space
Let us not fall, for he is merciless and hungry to devour
The devil is brutal, ruthless and destructive
He is cruel, greedy and has no feelings

Let us thus deny ourselves worldly pleasures
Let us deny ourselves worldly ill gains
And look up to the Lord for guidance
Let us devote our time to the Lord
Let us run our mile in the journey to heaven
And the lord will do the rest

Days are coming,
Seasons also as though in a race
This signals the coming of the Lord
The Lord is coming
Thus we should sacrifice all

Let us give our best to the Lord
The best in the quality of service
The best in time devoted
The best in giving and tithes

For this will be a step towards the Kingdom
In the Lord we need to sacrifice

In the Lord we need to act our faith
In the Lord we need to have hope
In the Lord we need to put our trust
And we will know why we have to sacrifice

With our hearts and all that we are
With our wounded vanity or pride
Let us come to the Lord
Let us shun all worldly desires

And come judgement day
We will have our reward from the Lord,
As our record will be clean, convincing and true
Let us sacrifice today for the joy to come

Let us spend time in praise
In praise we see the power of the Lord
We talk to him, we meet him
In praise answers unfold, riddles are resolved
Broken hearts are mended
As real joy descends, untapped and in abundance

Give us power to close all steel screens around us
Make our big eyes blind to all worldly glitterings
For all that glitters…. Let us realise
Keep our eyes well focused
Give us power to put you before our plans
Power to say "God willing then…"

Surely it is when God willing,
That our plans unveil in the manner we want
In the manner our hearts cherish
But we are myopic
Our hearts do not see
Our eyes do not see
Our hearts do not realise
Our minds do not realise
Open up our understanding

Let us sacrifice our love
To be selfless
For love is your command
The greatest of all is love, make us understand
With this we will be the salt of the earth
We will be the unshadowed light of the world
And our neighbours will see God
Their hearts will come for life
With praises descending from mountain tops, valleys and
beneath the seas
And the people will be one, one voice, one mind and one
purpose

Help us Lord
To sacrifice all
To love honestly without deceit
To commit ourselves more than before
For now is the time for his return
And time up for the devil

The Star Of Bethelham

It shone years back to be our guiding light
Marking the birth of a King
The King who U destined to die
Warranting men's salvation
But many hardly understood

The King had come to bring life
But jealous and hate controlled hearts of many
And the King they killed
Yet the star had not come in vain
Even the death could not steal the power

As we celebrate his birthday today
With our hearts and all that we are
Let us not lose focus from our guiding principles
For his death which brought us life
Came only after his birth

The King had come to save his fellowmen
But some doubted he was the child of God
They abused, belittled, disgraced, harassed, tormented and killed
Yet three days after death his eyes were to open again
He rose from the dead
Being the only victor of death
A miracle that left many panickingly mute and dumbfounded

The star of Bethleham years now
Marked the birth of a King- a King of all mankind

The one who would be the redeemer, comforter, counsellor and prince of peace
The one who would bring salvation, peace and unity among races
The one who would be the bridge for man into eternity, prosperity and all
Thus our hearts are in total praise today

Our hearts are singing joyfully today
For the birth of the King- the King, Lord Jesus
Was an important happening to us
Bringing us peace, joy and harmony
It brought us out of wicked ways
It brought us out of the dark world
And today our praises go to him-our King
For indeed He is worthy honour and praise
No one, nothing above or beneath seas compares
The star of Bethleham was mighty
And still is today

With the love He manifested
With the sacrifice he showed
With the suffering he endured
Today we stop to say " Glory, Glory to the King"
The King brought us life
Today we stop to say "hosana, hosana, hosana in the highest"

As we celebrate Christmas today
Let us give ourselves unconditionally to him
Let us live our lives purposefully in unison with the Lord

Let us deny ourselves the worldly glitterings, joys and sweetened
Deceiving ways
Let us live in a Christ like manner
And our Saviour will stop to say "son I'm impressed, well done"
For you are celebrating, with an understanding
Let us praise and worship as we honour his birth
Let us recommit, rededicate, reconfirm our love for him
And he will only be willing to let blessings descend forth

As we celebrate today
Let the spirit guide us
Let the power of God redirect us
Let us remain well-oiled and functional in the Lord
For the end is about

Let us praise without deceit
Let our hearts love without pretences
Let our hands avoid unholy deeds
For with you our purpose will be realised
Thus during this Christmas
Resuscitate our lives dear Lord
For you are the answer to our all-time worries and problems

Your Success Is Our Success

Our hearts share your joy today.
For the strides so giant, remarkable and commended
Strides coming with sacrifice and dedication
Strides coming with determination coupled with discipline

Our hearts wish you well today
An example to those coming up you have been
We wish you well brother
And may the Lord, our God
Be your guiding star
And his word and teachings your guiding principles

Our hearts wish you well today
And may all your dreams translate into life
May all your wishes unfold as you desire
Our hats are off to salute you, brother
Thus today on, do not look back

Our hearts wish you well dear brother
And wherever the wind blows you to
Remain our true ambassador
Wherever the world takes you brother
Let the Lord be your guiding light
And boast of his capabilities and abilities

Let no world corrupt tendencies impair your vision
Let no short cuts creep into your world
Let no crow flys deceive you
Always fight to the end in this harshy world
In this trying and tempting world

For on your side is the Lord

Let the greedy world not prostitute your mind
Let no material gains derail you values
Let your colours show to the wolves around you
Remain on guard for their imminent attack,
Be yourself always
And continue to bring us honour, happiness
We are now looking up to you, brother
And as up the ladder you go REMEMBER US

Real Love And Devotion

Real love knows no king no country
It knows no war nor pain
Real love knows no colour and puts no significance to it.
It knows no fights nor pretences
Real love knows no ills and back bites.
But devotion, faith and peace.

This is my song this summer
The song of love and devotion
For real love knows no wealthy nor poverty
It knows no class nor superiority.
Real love accommodates all, even weaknesses.
It resists the test of time and strong sweeping winds.
And critics wonder.
Yes this is love and devotion
Which is my repeated song this summer
Real love lives and grows by day
It encourages and conquers all
Real love transforms life
And translates all hopes
Real love and devotion should descend
And change the hearts of many
Hearts deceitful and uncaring.
Such care that comes with love.

This will be my all time song
For love is the greatest of all.

Praise

In the rain, in the cold
At noon, dusk or dawn
At all times - times of our lives
Keep praising the Lord
For in praise, we meet God
And feel his touch in our lives.
In praise he answers and gives hope.

Love For A Friend

To love is to do the best for a friend
With no eyes for anything in return
To love a friend is to be selfless
And have beast foolery buried.
Buying at no price the heart of a friend
And make him the prize of your heart
And vow never to hurt,
And take upon it to hate all ill winds,
Thus guard jealously your gourd of love
Given to you by your God at no price
And your prize will be abundant life

That when you abuse you fall head ward
And the test you will have drastically failed
Such drama imminent in our lives today.

Bleeding Heart

With immeasurable pain of loss
As seasons painfully prick our hearts,
Our comfort descends realising
You did not die in vain
As we look back in time Ruth
Our hearts profusely bleed
The thought of your loss is unbearable
But rest in peace

You were loving and caring
And our memories will always live
For you are irreplaceable Ruth
April 9 in 1999 appears just yesterday.
For the wound is still fresh.
Rest in peace

You were dependable and a shoulder to learn on
You had time to listen and lend a hand
Thus when we look back in time Ruth
Our hearts bleed profusely
Our hearts bleed endlessly
But today we are saying Rest in peace

We loved you Ruth
Your father, mother, brothers and all
Thus as you lie there peacefully
Remember we loved you dearly
We cherish the sweetness you brought us
We cherish the brilliant moments we shared

We cherish the person you were
But today as we glare into space
Remember we cared, we loved
But the Lord's programme only him knows
The Lord's programme only him can defer
Rest in peace Ruth

In your last days at Kadoma General Hospital
The pain in your heart hardly could be concealed
The worry in our hearts you could see
Yet it could not be offset
With our wits, means and all
Little we could have done Ruth
The Lord's time was up
As you lay in that bed
Your heart bleeding, ours too
This you could see Ruth
Today we can only say rest in peace

In May 1963 Ruth the baby came
Illuminating all candles in our life
Bringing us abundant joy and happiness
But little did we know Ruth
That so soon we would be robbed
That just at 36 you would go
That just that soon you would die
That baby Ruth would be Ruth the late so soon
But rest in peace

You were our pillar Ruth
As we look back in time
Inevitably our hearts bleed with pain

Our tears corrode our cheeks
You left a gap that will perpetuate
Rest in peace
Rest in peace Ruth.

A Call To Mama

At the genesis of my life
During all stages of development
During difficult and trying moments
You were there mama
Pain at times you experienced
Sleep at times you lost
Lond distances at times you walked
But today, tall I stand
You made me mama
You sacrificed for me mama
And my heart appreciates and salutes you
Be blessed with many days

Poverty Paralysis

Poverty paralyses and tantalizes
Indeed torments and tortures
Particularly women, all women
Who history has marginalized since time immemorial
History in patriarchal societies
Has been unkind to women
And the girl child is wailing today
Groaning, perturbed and in disarray

Poverty effects have been unkind
Yes, they have been far reaching and biting
Serenity in homes has varnished
Yet there has been a need for a remedy to the malady
There has been a need for a solution to the challenges
The myriad challenges caused by poverty

Like an answer to a prayer
Kuyedza women's club has come up with programs,
initiatives, and efforts
To guarantee serenity and sustainability in police homes
Kuyedza has empowered, capacitated police wives
with enterprising and enduring skills

Kuyedza has risen high in all seasons,
With programs well-conceived and executed,
Programs well developed and thought
so that poverty flees away
so that poverty waves bye to police families.

Kuyedza is, Kuyedza has been
The pillar to the emancipation of police wives,
Emancipation from the evil hold of poverty

Poverty can ravage the serenity in homes
Poverty has capacity to destroy homes
But Kuyedza descended as the answer that fosters peace
The only answer that breeds and sustains skills
Skills that will cultivate ingenuity
Progressiveness and innovation
Skills that grow incomes in all seasons
To ensure and guarantee peace, harmony
And purposefulness in police homes

With Kuyedza…
With the Kuyedza women's club
Poverty can never be embraced
With Kuyedza…n…
With the Kuyedza women's club
All police wives and families will never be the same
With Kuyedza…
With Kuyedza women's club
Poverty will shy away in police homes

Kuyedza Women's Club Bridging The Gap

The life in poverty can be painful,
Pain that ravages the serenity in homes,
Homes that we built in pursuit of love,
Harmony and tranquillity
Starving and peace are pole opposites to address
Thus Kuyedza came as the only intervention

Kuyedza came as the only intervention
The intervention committed to bringing peace
And food on the table
The intervention committed to providing
          skills to police wives
Skills that will usher unparalled
Transformation in our lives
Lives of the police families

Kuyedza has come to bridge the gap,
And the lives will surely change,
Police families will never be the same
There will be food on the table,
Incomes will be guaranteed
And this is the expectation of all homes

Poverty disturbs peace in homes
Poverty breeds conflict in families
But Kuyedza came to mitigate
And the lives of police families are
          set to improve
Yes, improve by day
Which is the wish of all mothers?

All mothers in families

Poverty can affect families,
Bringing in unnecessary fights
Because a hungry man is an angry man
Kuyedza will address this,
Kuyedza is addressing these problems
And indeed the quality of life will improve,
Improve by day,
Hats off to Kuyedza Womens' Club

HIV/AIDS A Sad Reality

A sad reality it is
Yet it has ravaged virtually all communities
Many families are in mourning today
Mourning for the loss of their beloved ones
Loss arising from the effects of HIV/AIDS

HIV/AIDS is sending shock waves
Yes, across all communities
Many have fallen victim
Some innocently….
Some by choice
Some by circumstances
Whatever the situation HIV/AIDS brings pain
Pain so real… pain you can almost touch
This is the kind of pain AIDS brings

People of the world HIV/AIDS is a reality
A sad reality indeed
In all seasons. Summer, autumn winter and
Spring let us remain conscious
For HIV/AIDS is upon us, and we will perish should we
fail to join hands

Efforts being pursued require our commitment
You and I can help deal with HIV/AIDS
Which is so rampant now
Yes in our own way.

Let us observe the ABCs of AIDS
Yes, abstinence, being faithful and using condoms

This will help mitigate the incidence of this scourge

Please my partner be there for me
Be responsible and exercise self-restraint
For HIV/AIDS is a sad reality,
You will die… I will die also
These kids… they will die also
Your other sexual partners will die also
Please!!! Please!!!
My partner HIV/AIDS is a sad reality
Let us remain faithful in all seasons
[*Won a prize during the Provincial Kuyedza Mini Show presented by Mrs Chingozha*]

Printed in the United States
By Bookmasters